WE
SANG A
DIRGE

LO ALAMAN

WE SANG A DIRGE

POEMS, LAMENTS, AND OTHER
THINGS THAT MATTER TO GOD

We Sang a Dirge Copyright © 2020 by Lo Alaman

All rights reserved. No part of this publication may be reproduced, stored in a retrieval system, or transmitted, in any form or by any means—electronic, mechanical, photocopying, recording, or otherwise—without prior written permission, except for brief quotations in critical reviews or articles.

All Scripture quotations are from the ESV® Bible (The Holy Bible, English Standard Version®), copyright © 2001 by Crossway, a publishing ministry of Good News Publishers. Used by permission. All rights reserved."

Printed in the United States of America

Cover design and layout by Strange Last Name

Alaman, Lo, 1992-
  We sang a dirge : poems, laments, and other things that matter to God / Lo Alaman. -- Franklin, Tennessee : Seedbed Publishing, ©2020.

   pages ; cm.

   ISBN 9781628248456 (paperback)
   ISBN 9781628248463 (Mobi)
   ISBN 9781628248470 (ePub)
   ISBN 9781628248487 (uPDF)

   1. Grief--Religious aspects--Christianity. 2. Grief--Poetry. 3. Christian poetry. 4. Laments--United States. 5. Race relations--Religious aspects--Christianity. I. Title.

BV4909 .A42 2020   248.8/6   2020947216

SEEDBED PUBLISHING
Franklin, Tennessee
seedbed.com

CONTENTS

Preface 7

PART ONE:
LEANING IN

Anew. 13
For Jeremy Mardis. 15
Casting Cares 17
House Rules 18
Song of Submission 21
The Prodigal Translates the BLM Protest 23
To Pray/To Speak 24
'20. 25
And Now . . . What? 28
Increase/Decrease. 30
Songs the Delivered Will Sing 31
N Words We Weren't Allowed to Say 33

PART TWO:
LAMENTING WITH

Post-Traumatic Stress. 41
In Search of Bright Sides and the Men That Stole Them 45
When Protest and Prayer Are the Same Song 47
Today We Say Enough. 49
Different Shades. 50
Cynicism 51
Another One 52
From Slaves to Exiles 53
If These Should Hold Their Peace. 54
Landmarks—A Black Church Tale. 55
Black on Black Crime and the Grieving Christ 57
Epiphany 58

PART THREE:
LISTENING TO

Turn to Your Neighbor and Say, "Jim Crow" 65
Praise Break—An Episode of Black Worship 68
Joy in Spite Of 71
Reunion 72
Strangers and Stargazers 75
And Then . . . Pain 78
Thank You, but No Thank You 79
Resilient 81
An Ode to Mothers 82
Sharpening Iron 85
Ora 86
Battle 88

PART FOUR:
LONGING FOR

Zion, Part One 93
Revival amidst Riots 94
And Then . . . Freedom 96
Prayer against Racial Divides 97
From Whence Mercies Flow 100
Ruah 101
Zion, Part Two 102
Pentecost 104
And Still . . . Hope 106
Informal Invitation 107
Luminous 109
Zion, Part Three 110

PREFACE

Ahmaud Arbery was gunned down the day before my twenty-eighth birthday. A few weeks passed and Breonna Taylor was killed on the same day that my daughter turned one. I didn't learn of either of these stories until they both garnered national attention later that May. Around that time, many of my white friends began to text and call me, to offer their condolences or ask for my opinions. Each conversation brought an opportunity to share the grace and truth of Jesus; to offer the good news as an alternative to the polarizing narratives of the day. I took every call.

When the video of George Floyd's murder went viral, my phone could barely stay charged. I spent the better parts of my day discussing systemic racism, the history of policing in America, racial reconciliation, and what role the church ought to play in all this. By the time the protests and riots began, the tone of the phone calls changed quite a bit. Some came seeking perspective. More came to share the perspective that their political ideology had already solidified. The work was tiring, but I'd committed myself to loving God and His people. Being available seemed like the first logical step in that direction. So I welcomed the exhaustion and bought a phone charger for my car.

I was invited to be a part of numerous panels. I got to jump on a few podcasts to talk about hard things pertaining to race. In the time of quarantine and the rise of Zoom meetings, there was no shortage of opportunities to step into these conversations. Conversations that I'd longed to have. For years I'd been heartbroken by the church's silence on issues of racial injustice and its complacency with homogeneity in worship. I'd been studying, praying, and waiting for a time when Christians would be ready to deal with this division in our culture, or at least address where it exists within our congregations. Finally, it seemed like we were at a point where these issues couldn't be avoided, and we'd be forced to deal with the mess we'd tried to sweep under the rug.

One day, I was on a call with a group of older white men in my church. They'd asked me to come and share my experience with them as a black man in America. Fortunately for them, I'd spent the last several months sharing my perspectives on the racial tension in our cultural moment and how I think Jesus is calling us to respond to it. Fortunately for me, that's not what they were interested in. "Thanks for the history lesson. But we were wanting to know how you feel." And just like that, I realized that I'd been sweeping my own feelings under the rug this whole time.

I'd been asked what I thought before I had a chance to process how I felt. And when asked how I felt, I'd placed reason in the place of emotion. I began to realize how this way of thinking had influenced my ministry. I'd made myself available to hear out the thoughts of anyone who called, but rarely did I ask them how they felt. When responding to their arguments, I tried to offer a more nuanced perspective and hopefully point people to Jesus. But my primary tool for this was to counter perspective with perspective, or facts with facts. I was trying to let information do a job that only compassion could do. The more I've wrestled with this notion, the more I'm convinced that this is what's happening in most of our culture, and it's why we're not getting anywhere.

When describing the generation of His day, Jesus said that it was as if children were playing music in the streets, yet the passersby wouldn't dance. They were like kids singing funeral songs in the marketplace, yet none would mourn with them. It isn't clear if the issue within this community was an inability to celebrate the joys and lament the burdens of others, or an unwillingness to do so. Either way, Christ's critique of apathy is explicit. Compassion has a job to do. And since arguments don't seem to be getting us anywhere, I'm hoping that a generation filled with the Spirit of God might respond better to the songs of those in mourning.

It is my belief that the cries of the black community have been and continue to be an echo of a deeper groaning (Rom. 8:19). The calls for justice, the will for unity, and the longing for our lives to matter all stem from and reach toward the God who made us in His image. And though

I hold that conviction closer to my heart now than I ever have before, I've retired from spending countless hours arguing to that end. After my conversation with that men's Bible study, I've sat in my own lament and let mourning take me to the Father's heart. This book is my attempt at condensing the racial tension and the unrest of black community, as well as my own, into a song for the marketplace.

What you hold in your hand is not a manual on lament, but rather a glance into mine. It is a collection of poems, journeys, prayers, and invitations. I offer no answers here, for only Christ has those to give. Poetry doesn't seek to share facts, but rather to share an experience. You'll find no politics or advocations for any government except the kingdom of God within these pages. Instead, I give you a window into the joy and grief of following Jesus in this skin. I pray these poems are a catalyst that open all sorts of windows (hopefully your own). Biblical lament stems from hope that God has more in mind for His people than the brokenness that they find themselves in. I pray these poems are a window into hope for you, as they have been for me.

Calling people "fam" has become a bit of a habit I've developed over the years. I hope this book, if nothing else, glorifies God as Father, portrays me honest as a human, and shows you that in Christ, we're kin.

Blessings, fam.

PART 1

LEANING IN

"Bear one another's burdens, and so fulfill the law of Christ."
GALATIANS 6:2

ANEW

Laid down here
Are leftover wants and tattered dreams
The rot of old and decaying desires
But I'll not weep

Here my heart is set on new affections
Here my fallen walls have been recycled into something much nicer
A new song migrates from my belly
Gains volume as it heads toward a frontier of voice
Carves a path right through my heart on the way
And makes no excuse for the mess it leaves

Find me,
Surprised by the image of self not covered in shadow
Fully awake with no lack to lay claim of me

Redemption is a holy thing
What does praise look like now?

A child's palms
Arms held high in longing toward a willing Father

A reaching heart
Every beat chasing presence
Seeking a love I once ran from

To recycle is to let go of what was
It is putting purpose up for auction
And laying our paddles down in surrender
Confession comes easy when we allow grace to outbid shame

To admit the sins of this nation
Is to make room for a better dream
It is to repurpose our loyalty toward a Kingdom over a government
And what does praise look like now?

A diverse hallelujah
Rainbows jealous of how we make color sound so harmonious

A peace among saints
Churches crying hosanna in unison
Lions laying down with lambs
Elephants and donkeys following suit

A fresh anointing
An on-time worship
Laid down here are old desires
Behold,
He does a new thing
Perhaps it's time we sing a new song

FOR JEREMY MARDIS

Oh son,
young and sweet fruit.
Did the bullet have a taste for you today?

Tell me,
was your skin not
the armor they thought it was? Five shots pierce you

easy.
Six years living.
You died a million heartbeats too soon. Dear child,

did they
forget this fight
was not with flesh and blood? Did they believe that

darkness
would be biased,
and spare your kind of flesh and your kind of blood?

Did they
believe the badge
holy? Like it would pardon your killers' sins

for them?
Clean as never.
Innocent as always are. As they always

will be.
What other grim
profession can call murder its target, and

its tool?
Poor slain body.
Cursed is the world that already had caskets

your size.
Fit you brown-boy
perfect. But where was the hashtag to lay your

name in?
All lives matter
spoke no words of your memory. Shed no tear.

Their mouths,
preoccupied
with cumbersome arguments. No room left for

mourning.
For lamenting.
For speaking of you, who died such a black death.

Oh child,
c'mon round here
now. Your name gets a seat at the spade table.

Your name
gets a plate at
the BBQ. We'll call you ours if they won't.

Welcome
to this ugly
club, of names grieved only by us and heaven.

CASTING CARES

Let's be honest
Let's not pretend this isn't ugly
When it is

I promise
You can call pain by its name
Without wounding your tongue

You can confess your fear
Without forfeiting your faith
Or offending your Father

He won't run away
He wants to hear
Tell Him all about it

HOUSE RULES

We stack cards in Uno.
Get caught slipping, and you might find yourself drawing all night.
Don't worry, we'll wait.
And ain't no trust among us so you gotta count each one out loud.

In Monopoly, trades are in no ways limited to the actual game.
I once convinced my little cousin to give me Park Ave.
    for taking dish duty that night.
This isn't cheating. It's good business.
Don't be a hater.

Spades stick around here.
You need ten to score in bones.
We do not encourage violence but spoons is a big kid game
And you've gotta do what you've gotta do sometimes.

We know these edicts are only canon here.
My fingers can trace the lines that border our sovereignty.
On another side of town, I hold playing cards like a collection
    of passports.
Grateful for the friends who share their space and customs with me.
Endure my trash talk and call me kin.
Teach me your ways and take these L's.
I'll gain mine elsewhere, I promise.

I love house rules.
It's proof that joy is a law in every home that has them.
They are a witness to the formula for gladness
Families mine out of spending time together.
Evidence of just how malleable a rule can be among loved ones.
Soft metal handrail, more guidance that governance.
Fruit of Spirit, against such there is no law.

Who can fashion laws in a home they don't have keys to?
Ask the culture to name its parents and they'll tell you
   whose house it is.
My praise fills a temple that welcomes every shade of child
The Spirit and womb can think up between them,
But I know the songs I will and will not sing today.
Know which outfits God has no problem with,
But my church won't let me preach in.
Which burdens my brothers and sisters want to carry with me
And which prayer requests are considered contraband to their ears.

I am more welcome than my culture is.
Praise God for an acoustic guitar, but what if my feet get light?
Amen for contemplation, but where do I put the fire and the shout
   I was raised in?
Amen for context, and tradition, and the other way around.
Amen for house rules,
But who's house is it?
And where do we expect the pieces of self that we're
   uncomfortable with to find shelter?

Can we try playing another game?
Can we swap this tiresome gamble out for something else
   that's a lot more friendly?
More humane than weaponized bias?
Misguided gravity within us
Indecipherable algorithm embedded in the amalgam between
   our faith and our politics.

Y'all tasted the sandwiches.
A greyhound couldn't find the competition.
Popeye's made Chick-fil-A look like an inexperienced dad
    packing lunch for the kids.
And yet, loyalty wouldn't let some call it what it was.
Y'all saw the footage.
I'd wager you heard the outcries long before,
But a pact with ideology, or party, or country
Charlie Browned your ears
To any sound that might mature your empathy.

To want my skin but not my voice is to hunt for pelts.
Representation without life is a funeral at best.
Don't invite me to the table if you don't care what I want to eat.
Or put more simply,
Remember who invited you to the table
And whose house this is in the first place.

Apathy leads nowhere near heaven.
I am no sore loser.
Game night is a holiday in my calendar no matter how it plays out.
Just need to know whose rules we're playing by.
If it be God's, then I'll bring every piece of me that I know grace
    can carry.
I'm learning just how malleable I can be in His love,
But if culture, tradition, or politics are governing our gathering
Y'all go ahead.
I'll sit this round out.

SONG OF SUBMISSION

White flags
Signature stamped to peace treaty
Defenses and arms laid down
Or arms held high in capitulation
This is surrender, as best we know it
This is farewell to the fight
I have nothing left to give
After giving it my best shot
This is the echo of an empty chamber
The sound of heavy breathing
After running out of options
Until there's only You
Until lesser choices fade from our sight
And Your love appears
Welcoming as the warmth of Spring
Our own strength melts away as feeble as snow
And I remember being here
I remember the feeling of captivity being slowly forgotten
Remember the thoughts that said there was no way out
Being silenced as I walked through one
I remember scars becoming vacant lots
With no pain to make a home of them
My healing,
Be the history books of Your faithfulness written on skin
My hands,
Be the flag raised high in the victory You've won for me
My signature,
Be the new name You claim for me as Your son
My song,
Be the echo of an empty chamber

Of arms laid down and arms saluting the sky
For You fight for me
And if You are for me
Who can be against?

THE PRODIGAL TRANSLATES THE BLM PROTEST

With pierced hands
He held our hearts secure
With blood-stained skin
He wiped our slate clean
To Him,
Healing fit best on wounds worn honest

Asking
Is the only hurdle receiving has to leap
Who better to cry out for justice than the oppressed?
What is pain if not a voice crying out in the wilderness
"Make straight the path for healing"?
What is a riot if not the ache of cities
Realizing that they are not heaven?

There's more than enough pain here
This is what far from home feels like
Our protests are coded cries for a Father
To us,
The unrest seems like a meal amongst swine
To Him,
It must feel like a time to fatten the calf

TO PRAY/TO SPEAK

Closed eyes ain't always the blindest
Nice words ain't always the kindest
Moses had to challenge Pharaoh
Christ had words with Pilate
Protests need no volume
Unless the problem is the silence
If sin still lynches those before us
Then these issues can't be behind us

There's a brief union between hammer and nail
Any longer condescends the effort
Is the need for awakening not an urgent build?
Do we not thirst for springs in the desert?
Perhaps the church forgot that peace is a tool
What is complacency but hoarded comfort?

Have we held our voices unmercifully long?
Will we quench the Spirit any longer?
Does the loss of God's children not ache us?
Is it time we cry out for the Father?

'20

What a year
What a collection of weeks we've had to wade through

What day is it anymore?
I admit, I've lost track
Too busy keeping count of all the loved ones I haven't seen

They're here, but they're not

Distance only makes the heart grow colder
To be sheltered in our places
Surrounded by isolation
We've never seen a disease wreak havoc in so many different ways
Quarantine threatens to take what the virus can't reach

We're here, but we're not

Been wearing hand-me-down smiles from last year
2020's been generous with burdens
I don't know how much more I can take
Depression is a hungry beast, roaming freely
Hard to keep convincing it that I am not a snack
Hard to keep convincing this country that our skin is human
That my blood
Owes nothing to the ground
Will water no seed
Still we watch
Our lives spill onto a land that don't know how to call us miracles
Still watching our kin slain
Still young
With not enough trips around the sun to learn the nuance of seasons
We watch them turn to lifeless droughts
Dust of lungs
Scorning the inhale that never came

They claim they can't breathe

We're here, but where are we?

Is this the world we've known?
Is there a normal left for us to go back to?
A place where peace still flows
Can it douse the fire of rage?
What hope can dam up the eyes
And keep these tears from falling?

Perhaps not ...
Perhaps there's no normal for us to return to
But we can build one

Our desire for change firm as bricks
Our longing for community the mortar

We'll see graves turn to gardens
Distance turn to runways
The phrase "I miss you"
Turn to "glad you're back"

We will call this anguish the flame that it is
And use it
To set anything that tries to divide us ablaze
We will brand ourselves in love
Hatred will not fuel this fire
Night will come,
But darkness will not claim our morning

Pain won't claim this year
2020 will be remembered
But we'll decide what it's remembered for

They'll remember that we were here
That we didn't fall apart, but stood in unity
They'll remember that we were here

That we wouldn't be silenced, and our voices were catalysts for change

They'll remember that we were here
We were here
We were here
We were here

And we brought a future with us

AND NOW ... WHAT?

Is it a movement if we go nowhere?

Amen to the white friends who have joined in on the prayer line
Amen to the blacked-out photos that hang like a curtain
    over your social media platforms

Praise God that the protest was seasoned with as much salt
    as it was pepper this time around
We sent directions
Glad to see y'all finally made it
White folks showed up on CP time

But what matters most is that you're here
So what now?

If we're committed to walking together
Where are we heading, friend?
How will we know to call this ground a road
If we don't know the language of destination to ask its name?

Is a bridge not a conversation between two places?
Have we put more thought into what we should or shouldn't say
Rather than where we want to go?
And who we want to be?

Eleven-year-old me is arguing with my older sister
    over the remote control to the TV
Our fight turns physical
And she hits me upside the head with a phone book

I lose the battle
Mom comes home from work hours later
And I show her the imprint of numbers of all of our neighbors
Whose names begin with the letter H
Branded on my forehead

I win the war
Raven is sent to her room
And I hold the power of over two hundred channels in my palms
I have overcome
I have endured
I have forgotten what I even wanted to watch

A new power courses familiar through the church's veins
The kind of power that only comes
When the comfortable have decided that discomfort
    is a more worthy casualty
Than the oppressed and marginalized around them

The church is deciding to awaken
To die to complacency like Christ died to sin
There's a kingdom coming amongst neighbors
Who are committed to bearing one another's burdens

What will we watch?
What kind of community do we want to see?
It's not a movement unless we go somewhere
So where to, friend?

Even the smallest step toward somewhere worth going
Is considered a journey

INCREASE/DECREASE

Christians be midnight ignorant
Swear we so bright
We ignore the main lesson the day tries to teach us
That the brighter we allow the sun to get
The more our own stardom must vanish
And ain't this glory?
Ain't it hope beyond our own brilliance?
What our world truly needs?
A new morning

SONGS THE DELIVERED WILL SING

We do not sing for blank pages
Our praise is not reserved for quiet stories
We don't praise the days because they are void of chaos
We do not celebrate the moments simply because they go so well
We celebrate them
Because soon after they will be raptured into memory
And this is how we create peace
This is how we give the mind some joy to call on
In the moments
When despair seems to have ravaged whatever earth our hope
    once stood on

So yes

Praise God for the struggles
And the testimony He makes of their tombstones
Praise the heartache
And the place it holds on His résumé
As previous experiences that qualify Him for the job
Praise God for the storm
That His sovereignty turns to mortar
His faithfulness lays the bricks of "peace, be still"
That my confidence is now built on

Smiles can be heavy
The weight of the world doesn't always sit easy on the shoulders
Sometimes my courage shows up late to work
When fear is right on time
Couldn't tell you how many times I've seen weapons form
But I can tell you
That we're alive today because they didn't prosper

So praise the Defender
The mighty fortress
That affords rest to the restless
And strength to the weakest
Praise the God who brawls on our behalf
Whose love is both bended knee, and bruised hands
Whether His proposal is an engagement ring
Or Him stepping into one
Praise His commitment
To the forever fight
Praise the God who fights for us

N WORDS WE WEREN'T ALLOWED TO SAY

1.

My boy Javon says
"Lo, that n*gga Jesus
Is turning my life around"

And I am an undone laughter
A guttural joy
Unhindered by diaphragm or decorum
My heart can't help but to call beautiful
What my westernized religion only knows how to perceive as blasphemy

Which is closer to the nature of Christ
I am not sure
Isn't this just what happens
When the Spirit touches a sinner's tongue?
Confession falls from the lips quicker than political correctness
    can catch

Pray we hear it more often
Pray that n*gga Jesus save all my n*ggas
Both the ones that can and absolutely cannot say n*gga

The latter will tell the former
That words like that don't belong in the Father's house
Call their vernacular contraband and miss the miracle it carries
Expect the tongue to be baptized before the body
Condemn the language
Of square pegs to fit their round hole comfort

2.

I mean, I get it,
I guess
White folks gotta take extra precautions when saying
    "knicker" and "snigger"
But what y'all using them words for anyway?
I get the unfairness of it
How come we get to regurgitate our favorite rap lyrics with impunity?
While white fans have to echo the genre with more skips than a
    scratched-up CD

I understand the sensitivity
History hit a pretty hard fork in the road
Words like that remind us of an ugly past
Filled with wrong turns and burned bridges
But still
Perhaps the labeled ain't been as liberated as the labelers
    would like us to believe

Among the murderers and deserters
Perhaps Christ has room at the table for potty mouths as well
And is even worthy of whatever broken praise they might bring to Him
On their tainted tongues

3.

N words we weren't allowed to say
No
Never
Not again
Nice day, officer
Our native language
Not forgotten
But stripped from our mouths like a smooth mouthed screw

N words we were made to feel
Numb
Nervous
Nasty
Negative about ourselves
Nooses
around necks
hung on trees
Watched loved ones go up, then down, then back up again
Like they were capitalizing the letter
As if the black body was a proper noun

But there were N words that we couldn't own
Like our Names
Like our Needs
Like the Narrative of what this country has done to us
Neighborhoods, free of violence
Here I speak of both Tulsa in 1921
And Fuller Park tonight

N words that we lost
Our Nerves
Our Newborns
Our Nieces
Our Nephews
Our N*ggas
Our N*ggas
Our N*ggas

4.

I make a poor handyman
My wife fills my toolbox with a list of numbers to contact professionals
Plumbers, electricians, and other people who actually know
    what they're doing
She's a hater
But I know she's not wrong

Still,
Even I've stripped enough screws to recognize
    where the church is heading
Vacant pews and hollowed saints
Repentance is a turning motion
But we demand it in advance with grinding force
Christ has a grace for my friends
That my church doesn't always know how to give

And this commitment to only presenting and accepting
    what is neat and polished
Is face value ugly
The underlying issue of calling black speech sinful
Is a hidden hideosity
Ol' busted face
Like you got hit in the face with a sack a nickels lookin' boy

5.

I imagine Christ as the brown boy He was
Slandered by names and accusations only He could repurpose

"Hail the king of the Jews" they taunt
"Isn't this the carpenter's son?" they mock
"He eats with sinners and tax collectors" they scoff

And He claps back
By preparing us a seat at the table He built in His kingdom
Sows seed in loose and rigid soil
Tells the harvest He has a home for it
Regardless of the type of dirt it was buried in

"That n*gga Jesus is cold"
Javon says
His statement rich in eschatological theology
A toddler faith taking its first steps
Toward walking in God's call for his life
He is learning to believe the promise of God is for Him
I dare not call this anything but beautiful

We gone call this grace, my n*gga
Now there's a word we all can use
White, black, or any shaded saint in between

When love meets us
Right where we are
Call it grace
As it is
As it's always been

PART 2

LAMENTING WITH

"Rejoice with those who rejoice, weep with those who weep."
ROMANS 12:15

POST-TRAUMATIC STRESS

Far from home
War welcomes us with violent arms
We rest our loyalty with those whose bodies are blanketed in the same uniform as us
We submit to those in command
Knowing each decision could potentially confiscate our heartbeat
We commit to serve our country
We know our role
We all fall in line

bang!

Enemies attack from every side
Bullets fly like horizontal rain
The storm is here and everyone is drenched
Those we've learned to call our own are taken from us
Where fight once preached within me
Has silenced itself and handed the mic over to survival
We just want to make it home
We know our wounds
We fall in droves

bang!

Our slain parade around us
We watch good men and women do unspeakable things
To keep their names alive
We drink it all in
Our tongues taste the bitter reality
That our stomachs will later call trauma
Until someone elsewhere remembers our humanity
And calls us home
We just want things to go back to normal
We know what we've seen
We all fall back in line

bang!

The car blows its horn and we duck for cover
Every shadow cast from a tree looks like limbs holding weapons
    intent to harm us
The steps you take tickle your spine with anxiety
When you fear every inch of your country is gardened with land mines
The enemy has hijacked our nervous system
We attack things meant to help us
We know the damage that's been done
We all fall apart

bang!

War knows how to end everything except itself
It doesn't conclude
It simply relocates
Bring the war zone to your chest and make you dodge
    breath like bullets
PTSD makes draft day of every situation
It is to be sworn in to night terrors
It's to pledge allegiance to flashbacks and the darkness of depression
We are home
But our minds have known nothing but violence
Are you shocked by the crime in our community?
Are you confused by our riots and outrage?
Are you surprised that this poem is not about the military?

bang!

Far from home
We were ripped from our country with violent arms
We rested our loyalty with those whose bodies were blanketed in
    the same color uniform as us
We submitted to those in command
Knowing each decision could potentially confiscate our heartbeat
We committed to serve this country
We knew our roles
We all fell in line

bang!

Those we called our own were taken from us
Our slain were paraded on trees, whose shadows still haunt us
    to this day
We tasted trauma and let fear tickle our spines
Until someone elsewhere realized our humanity
We sang of stars, spangles, and banners
We pledged allegiance to flashbacks and the darkness of depression
We knelt for flags
They knelt on necks
And asked "What about black on black crime?"
As if this war hadn't relocated into our hearts
As if post-traumatic stress doesn't cause an addiction to self-destruction

bang!

The black community knows PTSD
If there's a balm in Gilead
Could we borrow that for a while?
Let the church realize the war and know where to send its troops
Come brothers,
Come countrymen,
Let us lay down our old weapons
In favor of new ones
Too much damage has already been done
Let our pledge be to healing and understanding
Christ calls
We know our role

Let us all fall in line

IN SEARCH OF BRIGHT SIDES AND THE MEN WHO STOLE THEM

Look there

Just past the moon

A star, a light, an empty

Soon the sun will come, with all of its noisy friends

Enjoy this peace before it vanishes

Like shade in the brilliance of morning

Like my father, and his before

Where do all the black fathers go?

Several are spoon-fed to beasts called prisons

But I don't find mine in their jaws

Many are tied like a shoelace to streets

I've interrogated countless corners

And haven't heard a murmur of the man I'm from

Still others float aimless

Something in their DNA grown tired of being hunted

Won't place their story in the hands of something as deceitful as setting

As staying

The only consistent thing they've ever known is malice

Why wield such a thing against your own?

Why be anything other than midnight?

A beautiful absence

Room to grow

Space unbothered by assurance

I've learned to fail well

To fall without the safety net of a father's arms

Here I am

Defending the vacancy that guts me

Praying I never hollow my loved ones the same

Searching for a promise to end the day with

Searching for God in the night

WHEN PROTEST AND PRAYER ARE THE SAME SONG

Ain't the keyboard tired?
Ain't it sick of being forced to sound like something it isn't?
Ain't it sustained for too long?
Ain't its buttons been pressed too much?
Ain't it fed up with being a plaything for inexperienced hands?
Let it respond
Let it raise the volume on its frustration
Let the depths of its lament be transposed
To a key that silence can't lock up
Let it hurt out loud
Let it be loud enough for all to hear

What a beating the drum takes
How oppressive the sticks must seem
Could see one strike as coincidence
But how long before we call the cadence systemic?
How many blows can it take before it can't anymore?
Let it speak out
Let percussion come from its protest
Let it sound off
Let it push back
Let a rhythm be born of how many times it says no
And doesn't crack
And doesn't break
And still is

So tight the violin's strings are pulled
So firm its neck is held
So sharp the bow cuts along its vulnerable body
So agonizing it must be to be sawed into
Let it cry
Let its aching be an audible groan
Let the sound it makes unsettle whoever hears it
Whoever won't tune it out
Whoever will listen

I've known Life to be a sweet song
I've known Living to be a complicated sheet of music
I've known many to fear Christ to be a critic of suffering
Forgetting He too was a man
Broken into a sad song
His body
Laid into a silent tomb
His resurrection
An invitation to keep quiet no longer

The Father is a good Conductor
He has staff lines for hands
An honest space for us to place all of our notes
Whether beautiful or broken
I've sung many sorrows to Him
I've been a playlist of emotions
I cry out before Him time and time again
And each time
He listens

TODAY WE SAY ENOUGH

So far
There have been 218 days this year
And over 250 mass shootings
Meaning we've seen death more than we've seen morning
Meaning we've seen more sons buried than we've seen suns rise
Put so many hers in a hearse
We're running out of ground to cemetery the land
On a more than daily basis
We reach for our phones
And the screen hands us another death to swallow
We've buried the bodies of so many innocents in our eyes
That our eyelids are turning to tombstones
We speak of so many funerals
Our native tongue has become bilingual
We are fluent in both English and eulogy
And still
We struggle to find the words to say "no more" in both

No more

DIFFERENT SHADES

I hug my mother
And can't help but notice her warmth
Can't help but guess that the heat of her blood
Is a mixture of miracle and malice
Can't help but notice that the lighter tint of her skin
Hints at foul play
Somewhere down the line
Lines were crossed
Grandma got abused and granddaddy became an ancestor
My ancestors are both victim and villain
My people are both saints and sinners
Both in desperate need of grace
Such is true of your blood
Such is true of all who bleed

CYNICISM

I do not fear the blade
In a surgeon's hands, I know it means well for me
I do not fear its prick, its slash, its cut
If its aim is meant for something that ails my body
I do not fear the blade
I fear the hands that hold it
And so it is with the bullet
And so it is with the badge
And so it is with the country, and how it defines my humanity that day

Both the birds and the snakes that eat them lay eggs
I have learned not to call every wrapped thing a gift
Forgive my praise for showing up late to progress's party
Fault me not for withholding my optimism
Until I know what it intends to do with me

I do not fear the blade
In God's hands, I know it means well for me
But this nation has long rejected the Father's grip
So it was with me
So it was with you
So it is for all before grace washed us newborn innocent
And we were received into the Father's arms with mercy
As family
Told simply to confess and believe
Forgive me
But I will fear this land until it does both

ANOTHER ONE

See them
The ghost of our kin
Racing violently through their own stories
Crushing the pavement of lips
Praying their footage stays relevant
Competing to champion memory
Knowing that America only has enough bandwidth
To remember the name of one slain at a time
And to be lost in our minds is to be truly lost
Forever
There is no expiration date on the grief of them
Families and friends will hollow
Where the warmth of their loved ones once filled
They will remember what we forget
The gun will fire and a fresh race will start
New stories of slain black bodies will fight for our attention
The Olympics of eulogy will call the dead to their places
And we will watch
As they race to be remembered

FROM SLAVES TO EXILES

They took our names
And taught us not to miss them
Work for titles, they said
Look for labels, they said
Learn to fit in
Like a knife
Carving its way through flesh
Perfect fit
If you don't mind the damage
Perfect fit
If you ignore the blood
Ignore the sirens
Ignore the pain
Countless dreams
Die every day
And not one tear is shed
So many identities go missing
Without an alarm ever sounding
And we're left wondering
Whether we should mourn or not

IF THESE SHOULD HOLD THEIR PEACE

Will the rocks have to cry out for me?
Will my song be silenced beneath the earth?
Will my praise be kept like a secret amongst tombstones?
Is the worship of my life of any worth?

Are my hands raised as hallelujahs to heaven?
Or is it fear of being shot that shoots my arms toward sky?
Have we seen enough hashtags in darkness to form a constellation?
Have we seen so much black death, we just assume black dies?

Will the rocks have to cry out for me?
Is the empty tomb not a testimony we love?
Does the black body owe a debt the Son didn't pay?
Was the blood of our Savior not enough?

Must the story always cast country as hero?
Will the narrative always paint the slain as villain?
Why are we seen as guilty until proven innocent?
What came first, the video or the victim?

Will the rocks have to cry out for me?
Have the saints forgotten the language of tears?
Are my cries only considered when counting collateral damage?
Is riot the only sound that they hear?

Does the damage not outweigh the outrage?
Will we critique the protest or search for the pain?
Why is the most always demanded of the least of these?
Must the weak always be asked for their strength?

Will the rocks have to cry out for me?
Does the church have a cry for me?
Will Christ be a rock for me?
Oh Lord,
Be a Rock

LANDMARKS—A BLACK CHURCH TALE

Journey with me
It's 1876
And African American Baptist Church of San Marcos
Is being burned to the ground by the KKK
They're taking flame
Purchased by hard-earned hatred
And trying to turn the building into a mixed pile of ash
    and scorched receipts

What misery
Yet another community gets swallowed up in senseless violence
The assailants see the validation of humanity as a fleeting commodity
So they deny it in others
The congregation gathers for prayer
With smoke pouring into their chests
And wouldn't you decide
Which town to point your feet toward next?
How quickly would your legs run to the nearest neighborhood
That actually sees you as neighbor? As human?
How fast would your feet race to wherever racists aren't

But no,
They said their legs weren't meant to leave this fight, but to stand in it
Stand tall, stand strong, stand together for something worth saving

Hate bore flame
And left the land marked with horror for history
But when brothers and sisters stand together it creates
    landmarks of change

A landmark of grace,
Though it took decades
They rebuilt their walls even bigger, and still opened their doors
    for those in need

A landmark of hope,
When their enemy came back
Blacks and whites stood together with a collective "I wish you would"
    on their faces
They didn't back down

A landmark of love,
You can find a good story here
One where humanity is championed over fear
Where community is born from the joining of hands
And we see people as people
As our people

May our landmarks be the ones that remind us
Not only of where we've been, but of who we are
May love unite us
To stand resilient as a building fireproofed by courage
May we journey together
May we build together
Let us build a tomorrow
That flame cannot take

BLACK ON BLACK CRIME AND THE GRIEVING CHRIST

Despite what the hood says,
Death was not meant to be wished upon a hater
To have the same sorrowful sleep prayed over them
That was amened over me
Is a mockery of the cross

Despite what the news says,
Death is no dance
And no matter how much rhythm brown bodies seem to have
They should not be expected to learn it sooner than others

Despite what despair says,
Death has no victory
I have removed sting
I have trampled it under feet
I have overcome oblivion
I lived in the tomb
And in three days I moved out
Now if any carry my message
They are forwarded to my new address

Right into the arms of the Father

EPIPHANY

Epiphany:
When the man says he doesn't see color
He does not mean that he doesn't see me
What he means is he doesn't see the boy
The child that was raised in this skin
He respects the person
But ignores the tale of how he got here
Won't judge a book by its cover
But doesn't care to learn certain parts of the content much either
Agrees that we all come from the same Author
But wherever history threatens a paper cut
He feels that it is a page best avoided
Besides, don't we all read forward anyway?
Don't bookmarks just cause division?
#allstoriesmatter

Epiphany:
When the man says he doesn't see color
He does not mean that he doesn't see me
He just doesn't see the boy
Doesn't see the lessons America has taught him
How a television full of white heroes with white faces made
    a script of his mind
And taught him the roles that he could and could not play
The successful among his kind were those that could run and jump
    and sing and dance
And the black man always died first in the movies
So no wonder this is exactly what characterized his community
And ain't that how it is?
Predominate culture over subculture?
Majority rule even at the expense of the minority?
Multiracial and multiethnic are not the same thing

So just knowing someone of a different race is pointless
    if you lack empathy
Having friends in an assortment of colors
Means nothing if you always bleach the tough conversations
    out of your conscience

Thought:
When the man says he doesn't see color
It doesn't mean he's a racist
It doesn't even mean that he is a villain
It doesn't mean he doesn't see me
It just means that if he can't see color, then he can't see blood
So when an entire community complains about their wounds
He is left believing everything is fine
And he'll defend that
Say I thought we got over all this
Thought we buried that hostility with those who fought for your freedom
I thought we were cool
And he will mean it
He will not be sinister at all
He'll simply fight for his right to remain ignorant
Men fear what they don't understand
And he won't understand why the boy grieves
He'll try to convince him
That everything is fine
The man will try to crack a smile using the boy's teeth
And all this apathy will do more harm than good

Stereotype:
Black people can't swim
If someone is to die drowning
It will be the fault of whoever pushed them into the water
As well as anyone who chooses to ignore that the water exists
If they die
Choose to understand the boy's mourning

The man says he doesn't see color
But even he knows to wear black to a funeral
Can't he see that black grieves?
Can't he see the boy
Shaking in the skin he claims not to notice?
That black lives are forced to learn this story from
    a different perspective
Can't he see how much being color blind costs?

Revelation:
Once
I asked God if black lives mattered
He said . . . yes
And there were no buts
There was no political correctness
Or hidden agenda
Only an answer to a question about His love
I asked
Where's the church been in all of this?
He said the church is His bride,
And this wasn't the first time that she had been unfaithful
And that He had grace for even mistakes such as these

I see a young male:
Skin painted the same color as mine
But social circles have colored him a bit more target
I call him boy
With all the love I know how
I tell him, don't you know?
That you are infinitely more than what most say you are
And yet every bit the king that some fear you will become?
I say, don't you know?
That the whole universe and its Maker are crazy in love with you?
That even the sky is envious of your face?
Whole day goes dark just to look like you
Tell him as long as there is blood in your veins

And you feel the touch of earth at your feet you will be
  some kind of prince
And on the day when you leave here
When your beauty is no longer bound to the ground nor this body
You will see a new type of kingdom
Be dressed in a new type of hope
And the world will miss you
Like the miracle it took for granted
And they'll demand you back
But you'll say no
That you're too full of new sky to return the wonder of yourself to them
And you'll be gone
Leaving nothing but the stars to remind them

PART 3

LISTENING TO

*"A fool takes no pleasure in understanding,
but only in expressing his opinion."*
PROVERBS 18:2

TURN TO YOUR NEIGHBOR AND SAY, "JIM CROW"

It is hot this June
But Halloween can't wait
Black bodies are turned to ghosts in the streets
Black church claims that racism is a monster hiding in plain sight
White church is searching its closet for what to wear
To be black in a white church is a strange holiday
It is dress up and disguise
It is candy and compromise
It is the joy of projecting God's image among difference
And the shame of being a token
The fear of being an outfit that helps your congregation pretend
    it's diverse
When it's not

When an innocent black body turns lifeless
Masked friends come to trick or treat at my doorstep
Wanting something sweet
Begging me to affirm their costumes with sugar
A snack to mollify the shamefaced legacy of their skin
Put away the life rafts and reward the masquerade
Even though I know
That there's a drowning sibling behind this facade
And too many sweet words will rot the mouth and pull my brothers
    and sisters under
I know affluence and whiteness are cavities in and of themselves
And though ethnicity is real
Race is just a ghost story we've passed down for generations too long

To be black in a white church is to consider my home a haunted house
Must be,
Why ain't nobody from the church ever been over to visit?
Why am I invited more than my invitations are accepted?
Community is never on our land or our terms
But when has it ever been?
Equality was defined by those who intentionally withheld it
Segregation fled from schools
But found sanctuary in our sanctuaries
Diversity is a fact of heaven
But only a fairytale within our walls

To be black in a white church is to put a costume on my frustrations
Dress them up more neatly than I feel them
To be more holy than I am honest
More Protestant than protest
Keep the ratio between pleasant and outraged
Skewed in the favor of my company's convictions

Growing up
My church condemned Halloween
Called it the devil's day
Held a fall festival instead
Where we carved pumpkins, ate candy, wore costumes,
And did pretty much everything else you do for Halloween
Yet somehow was not

To be black in a white church
Is to do everything the same as everyone else
And somehow be not

Somehow
I will learn the songs of this home
And sing until house keys rattle in my throat
No one here will miss the songs of my culture other than me and God
Their loss, whether they know it or not
Another innocent black body will turn lifeless sooner or later
They will apologize to me
As if it's my burden to carry
And not ours

I will carve a jack-o-lantern smile across my face
And call it fellowship
They'll call this unity
I will serve this church faithfully
Praying its success
Praying its demise
Let it shatter into a million homogenous pieces
A puzzle of sameness
Nothing linking it together ever again

And from the rubble
Come a new house
One where everyone misses the ones not here
And names like black church, and white church
Become as useless as a coat in June
Leave autumn and its holidays elsewhere
Here we are together, dancing
All present and accounted for
Coming alive
Like we were always meant to . . .

Together
Truly. Together

PRAISE BREAK—AN EPISODE OF BLACK WORSHIP

The choir shouts
Voices wall together like perfectly laid brick
A warring cry
A violent union
Bids no devil welcome here
Church mother wails
Grapples fiercely with her Lord and calls down a blessing
Hollers a cry only labor could give
Her voice builds a birthing ward in the Father's house
Demands
That someone she loves will see His goodness in the land of the living
And where are the musicians?
Little Kevin is learning his limbs at the drum set
Each one swings in ways he never knew they could
And they never forgot that they were meant to
Uncle Andre is forgetting himself in a guitar
Buries his heart deep into the song
As if he'll meet the grandfather that taught him to play in each note
Tries to summon the corner of heaven his loved ones occupy
Into the room
The song brings the King instead
And no one is disappointed
Sister School-Girl gives her knuckles to the piano
Throws them at the keys like she'll never use them again
A fire catches inside her
And the music turns to flame
The whole house is ablaze now
A sweet fragrance rising

Everything not of this room turns to ash
Ebenezer and John P. Kee fill the firmament
My eyes drift over to Mr. Patton
Here he is no longer the principal who paddled my deserving behind
Back in the 7th grade
Here he is a page of Psalm
A hymnal of years and testimony
He will hug me after service
And I will remember that the sacredness of a black man's love
Does not make it a myth
The pastor finds the thunder in his voice
Tells us to go do what we cannot
And go be who we are not
Something unlike truth melts like wax
And falls off of our hearts
"But God" becomes a parachute
And we all feel the rush of leaping creep like an addiction into our souls
We will size up the cliffs before we part
We will be here for the largest of hours
Each one the size of a planet
The offering plate will orbit around more often than we can
    make sense of
Our prayers will chase the sick home
We lift their names with confidence and belief
It will be years before I realize that the "bereaved family"
Is not a household within our congregation that has perpetual
    health issues
Today we've seasoned the walls with our praise
The building will sit somewhat idle for a while
Until Sunday calls
Like a school bell to students, and sinners, and arsonists alike
Come Sunday
The fire will light again

We will bring our offerings
By grace
May even become them

And I was glad when they said unto me
Let us go into the house of the Lord

JOY IN SPITE OF

This is a glad day
There'll be no grey clouds
In this poem
Today,
I hold hands with
So many that I love
And for those that I love
Whose hands I cannot reach
Beneath the ground
I hold their memory
As Christ holds us all
No tears to be found
No dark clouds in view
Only my loved ones
And memories
And sun

REUNION

My family is a mixed treasure
One that is not easily found
But is one all the same
Come the holidays
We will fill someone's house
With too much laughter and too much music
The wisest of us will fill the kitchen
There will be no discussion about the alchemy that is to take place
All will simply know
All will simply do

The rest of us will pass the time with board games and old stories
Tales that make the treasure worth its weight
Like how Grandpa Milford was the only black man to curse out
    white folks in 60s
Without a bullet or fist learning the address to his body
Or how he'd take my oldest sister with him everywhere he went
On long drives through Southern California summers
Even to the bar with him
When she was only five years old
And no one in town ever questioned it

We'll speak of leather belts and their lessons we earned
Or the most elaborate ways we ducked bill collectors
Or the strange things we did to get by through the rough days
The ways we made sense of life
And found gladness
Even during the times that saw us less human than we've always
    known we've been

And an angel of the Lord will descend
And fall upon the house in the form of a sweet aroma
Something holy emanating from the kitchen
The Lord Himself will call to us from the pots
Will say "Come,
See this great thing Aunt Nita has done"
We flock like migrating birds
To the south of the dinner table
With eager mouths
We give thanks to the altruistic God who's provided us with the bounty
No one rushes the prayer
"Rise, Peter, slay and eat"

All of my uncles' lips are stained with their daddy's words
My sister is a bartender now
Each of our presents are shaped by our shared past
Our blood knows the river it comes from
The stories we pass down force an accent onto our voices
As if to remind us
That our lives will one day fit into the mouths of those we antedate
As if to say,
"Choose ye this day what kind of ancestor you will be"

The scent of loved ones will linger in my clothes for weeks
I will carry their warmth with me even longer
When the apostle Paul speaks of inheritance
I hear a family word
A tale passed down through blood
A treasure
Linking generations together
Close as kin

The story speaks
Of a great cloud of witnesses
A forecast of future family reunions
A choir of sibling saints passed before us
They sing
"Soon, brother,
You too will know the anchoring weight of a skeleton
And rejoice in the freedom of it
Soon, brother,
You too will see the image we were all made from
And call your neighbor kin
Soon, brother,
We'll all sit at the table
In our Father's house."

STRANGERS AND STARGAZERS

I am greatly amazed by all that we do not know
The mysteries of the heavens shrouded in our ignorance
The possibilities of intelligence outside of ourselves
Worlds that are not new
Only untouched by our knowing

On another planet
Galaxies beyond our understanding
Exists treasures that our minds wouldn't even know how to value
Beauties that our eyes wouldn't even know how to hold
Suppose they don't have races there
Suppose they found other means to unify the bodies
Discovered that harmony of crossing communities and cultures
That desperately eludes so many places on our planet
Suppose they found better use of pigment
Suppose they forged light from a totally different spectrum
A prism of reds, but not our reds
And blues, but not our blues
And colors that we don't even have words to describe
Creating lights that we don't have words to define
Perhaps the brown of my skin goes by a different name there
Perhaps this too is a treasure that our world has not always known
     how to value
But is beauty, all the same

On another planet
Not too far from my home
A mother ties the shoes of her son
With hands that should have been his father's hands
I believe his father to be on a planet like or near the one my father is on
Somewhere empty and safe from responsibility
Far enough away that they can't see the damage that has been done
The mother hugs her boy
But can't warm the chill of a fatherless world out of him
I have known such hugs
And felt them fail at such chills
But this is not my home
We are worlds apart
Although close enough to eat the same meals
To shop at the same grocery store
We look the same
But I do not share his gravity
The weight on his shoulders
Far more heavy than anything I could bear
His may be a story of violent pains,
Or drug abuse pains,
Or police brutality pains,
Or any other pains ascribed to brown boys on such heinous planets
And though I may share some similar pains
I am ignorant of more
My skin has never worn many of those bruises
And I mourn him as both a brother and a stranger with the same tears

Often
I am asked to speak on behalf of people and planets I've never known
Assumed
That one scar can make sense of another
Simply because they share the same shade of scab
To this end
I always prove useless
And to many others as well
Perhaps we are all looking for the same things
To understand our world
And the worlds of those around us
Perhaps this is not the job of scholars, or astronomers,
    or presumptuous stargazers
Perhaps we don't need any more maps, or books, or panels
Perhaps what we need are spaceships
And rockets

AND THEN... PAIN

How familiar
The thorn becomes to the flesh
How everyday the burden feels
Every once in a while
It bleeds over into the week
From time to time
A month of it
Sometimes
The season seems here to stay
Seems a jealous friend
That doesn't want to share you
Like you belong to it
Like sadness is written in permanent ink
How long
Before we call this abuse
How long
Before we stop hiding behind
"I'm okay"
How long
Before we cry out
And lament

THANK YOU, BUT NO THANK YOU

What I imagine is meant by "It'll be okay"
Is, "I sorta suck at comforting people"
Or, "At least I'm not giving you bad advice"
Or, "I really don't know what else to say,
But I want you to know that I care"

What I imagine is meant by "I know how you feel"
Is, "I'm a self-accredited counselor"
Or, "I didn't have enough time to Google what not to say
    to a grieving friend
Before this conversation"
Or, "I want you to know that you are not alone,
And I'm willing to share my story if it helps"

What I imagine is meant by "Be strong"
Is, "If you try hard enough, you won't be depressed"
Or, "I really want you to keep breathing, friend"
Or, "I know a wild despair may seem like a cute pet when it's young,
But when it grows older, it will want to run away with you
    in between its teeth,
And I love you too much not to voice my concern"

What I imagine is meant by "I'm here for you"
Is, "I want to be here for you, but I don't know how"
Or, "I want to be here for you, but the right words are as slippery
    as wet soap"
Or, "I want to be here for you, but I'm honestly not sure if you even
    want me to be"

And sometimes I don't

Sometimes "It'll be okay"
Sounds like "Hurry up and get over it"
Sometimes "Be strong"
Sounds like an impossible task
Sounds like
"Don't spill your sadness here"
"Don't stain my clean morning,
With all of your problems"
Sometimes I get in my head about these things
But sometimes
Comforting just feels uncomfortable

RESILIENT

Some days
I run out of happiness
Some days
All of my positivity fails me
And my words can't hold their optimism
And my lips can't carry
The weight of another forced smile
Some days
I am a foreigner in my own confidence
As if I don't have all the proper documents
To access my own strength
Some days I am weak
Some days
Joy forgets how to find me
As if this is not a place I've been
Countless times
Some days broken is the only way
That I know how to be
Some days I feel
Like this is all that I'll ever be
But praise God for the tutor that time is
For what it has taught me
Is that these days
Always end
And that so far
I haven't

AN ODE TO MOTHERS

When we were born
When we inhaled and our lungs held breath for the first time
And our eyes opened like two small prayers searching for grace
When everything was strange
So all we knew was faith
We were born believing in one thing
That life is a gift
In this poem
We honor the women that were unwrapped to give it
An ode to the mothers
An ode to the walking monuments of selflessness
You
Are one of the greatest treasures this world has ever known

Though the world may never fully know the weight of your crown
You are queen all the same
For the days that you sacrificed into night to brighten our tomorrows
For the many overtimes you clocked in to watch over us
Your love
Remained timeless even when we held back some of ours
You are strength
Strong enough to forge meals into moments
To turn any situation into a classroom
And raise children higher than the standards this world will try
    to ground into them

When I was a boy
I watched my mother go to war for our family
Saw her prayers battled back against statistics
While bearing the backbreaking weight of being a single mother
But her faith never faltered
She kept her composure like a good secret
And worked her fingers to the bone
To give everything but up on us
Ode to a mother's love
Be it the first example of God that we are shown
To graciously give of self to make another whole
To mirror a hope like the coming of a messiah
You are nativity
And one day the world will again be wisemen enough to recognize
    you as miracle

Sometimes we forget
That doing a good job doesn't mean it isn't a hard one
That though your task may be rewarding
That doesn't mean it isn't difficult
And a circus of circumstances
So when you feel like an opening act
When you are forced to juggle parenting and your sanity
    in the same breath
And walk a tightrope through life with an even tighter grip on your faith
Never doubt
That what you do is amazing
That having a child may change your life
But raising a child will change the world
And that we literally have no world without you

You are a promise
One that God intends to keep
You are more precious that a fistful of diamond
The more cuts you take the better His light shines through you
Your love
Is more home than any building dare to be
An ode to your light mother
For always being the place we can return to

SHARPENING IRON

What are brothers?
Are they men or myth?
Are they a loyalty that at times seems
Too good to be true?
Yet honest as the wounds you've earned together?
I am grateful for mine
They are a love that's been proven
They are the boys that became men with me
The men I wrestled with until our bond became strong
As iron sharpened by iron
If Christ be an anchor, and the world a sea,
Then my brothers are the relationships that kept me afloat
While learning how to hold on
We hold each other down, like the sky is against us
And we need this heavy of a love
To keep each other grounded
What is brotherhood
If not proof that we share the same blood without the need
Of spilling it?
The blessings that help build me into a man
These are brothers
I am grateful for mine

ORA

We have no pictures together
No bond we share canonized between pixels or frame
Curse the days, Ora,
For not making selfies sooner
Curse my age, Ora,
That races me reckless into such selfish corners
There is no shortage of seconds back home
Mississippi holds just as many hours as it ever has
And yet,
I never took the time to come see about you
Spent so much time learning the right way to minister
I forgot to honor the woman who first showed me how it's done
Curse my shame, Ora,
Can still hear your voice rebranding me a southern boy
Back when I had no roots
Used to joke about how y'all mispronounced my name
Before I noticed I was being planted as kin in the soil of your accent
I am who I am because of your home
Though I didn't appreciate it as much back then
Used to try to scrape your address off of my memory
And tell my story in a different setting
Trying to convince myself I was somewhere I wasn't
We chased so many different settings
Trying to convince ourselves we were someone's we weren't
You cried the first time you saw us dance
Proud to see us finally moving freely in our skin
I believe you believed God for us before we could
You cried the first time I preached
Said it was about time I stopped running from my calling
I never called to see about you
Curse my pain, Ora,
Guilt keeps trying to sit in gratitude's seat

To keep me from yet thanking God for the blessing you were
    to me and my family
But I'll praise anyway
I'll say I miss you now
And repent for not admitting it then
I'll think of your hugs and ache at their absence
While celebrating that God has you wrapped in His embrace
I will visit the home you opened up to us when we had nowhere to go
I will call you mother in my prayers
I will dance and preach and praise the God who was faithful
    to be with you when I wasn't
Curse the pain, Ora,
Bless the God who has taken yours away

BATTLE

The heart is the size of a fist
Vulnerability
Is a splayed palm
It is honesty at the tip of fingers
It is freedom at the expense of a loose grip

But who can fight this way?
Whose life isn't set up unsettled,
Every now and then?
Whose life isn't a corner store
Built on the sketchy side of town,
Sometimes?
How can you stay open 24/7
And not be prepared to defend yourself
From what the night may bring?

The first night I ever prayed to God
My eyes were shut tight
My fists were clenched even tighter
Ready to turn my bedroom into a boxing ring
To bob and weave
Away from any attempts at harming me

But He met me with an open heart
With His hands outstretched
Told me that He wasn't afraid of the fight I would bring
Told me that I can place the sharp ends of my brokenness
In the proof
Of His already pierced palms

I was not ready to give in
I swung my fist like clenched flowers buds
Blowing in the breeze
But God was patient
And still is
Springtime emanating from His optimism
Believes that I will bloom one day
Into a field of unguarded color
I pray it so
I pray it so
I pray it so

PART 4

LONGING FOR

"For to this end we toil and strive, because we have our hope set on the living God, who is the Savior of all people, especially of those who believe."

1 TIMOTHY 4:10

ZION, PART ONE

When we stand at the gates
Forever unfolding before us
When our broken hearts puzzle piece themselves whole
Into the perfect picture of God's glory
That they have all played a part in

When we unlearn fear
And we forget shame and all its vices
And our lungs fill with that first full breath of eternity

When our souls
Are washed clean of old names,
Without a syllable of sin left to stain them
And we are handed fresh new ones
That lesser tongues have never touched
And a new song syrups its way sweet onto our lips

We will sing

"So long, shadow
There's too much light here for you to follow
Goodbye pain
Love's too full here
There's no room for sorrow
Goodbye hurt, and harm, and fears
Goodbye tears
Our God has wiped you all away"

REVIVAL AMIDST RIOTS

Revive us, Abba
Tell the dead to try again

Reshape us, Abba
Point our pasts to where they end

Respond to us, oh Lord
We need to hear the words You say

Remake us, oh Lord
Turn our pillars back to clay

Reinforce us, Abba
We're forever stuck beneath this load

Refresh us, Abba
When we buy into the lies we're told

We pray You remind us, Father
That we were naked and free of shame

Recover us, Father
Clothe our hearts and strip our pain

Renew us, Lord
When we're more holy than we are honest

Rebuke us, Lord
When we want You less than Your promise

Reduce us, God
Make less of we and more of Jesus

Refuse us, God
If we seek country over kingdom

Review us, Shepherd
Search our hearts, and if they're off

Then please, rescue us, Shepherd
Till ninety-nine aches for the lost

Come reassign us, Lord
Commission us with flame and spirit

Let fire refine us, Lord
If buildings burn, make us empathetic

Would You restore us, Abba
To reflect the treasure that You've purchased

Would You reform us, Abba
And reinstate our lands with purpose

We need repentance, Jesus
Like blind eyes to racism we turn from sin

We need redemption, Jesus
For the Father of mercy to call us children again

We pray revive us, Abba
Don't let flame consume our story

We pray refine us, Abba
Use this fire for Your glory

We pray revive us, Abba
We pray revival, Abba
We pray, revive

AND THEN... FREEDOM

One day
Love will undo bondage
Freedom will call us by name
And the weight of whatever sin once claimed you
Will fall right off of your shoulders
And crack whatever ground it lands on
And you'll be so light
One leap
And the sky will catch you
Like a cloud
One day
We will all soar far above
Our chains

PRAYER AGAINST RACIAL DIVIDES

We are one in the Spirit
There are no colors on our souls
No pigments that have seeped deep enough to breach
    the depths of our hearts
For we were all born from the same shade of Your love
So,
May You make us after Your own image
May You, God, orchestrate this symphony of melanin to sing
    the beauty of Your face
May our faces be like music
May our colors compose a song that reflects every genre of Your love
Blending each of these skin tones into a melody that is too beautiful
    for one heart to sing
Form a choir
From the souls You've acquired from the grave
That we might sing Your name
And spring forth back into life as vibrant as the promise of Your rainbow
For You have paid the price for every nation and tongue
Who am I to segregate Your treasure?
Don't let it be so
That when the rooster Jim Crows
We deny the Christ who has called all sheep back into His fold
But instead
Give sight to these color-blind eyes
And make a home out of our lives
I pray that the rhythm of Your heartbeat
Quakes the very landscape of my worldview into loving those around me
Permit us to see just as You see
For You were always one
And always three
So we were always made in the very image of community
And called to worship as such
Just as the morning sun peels back the night's sky

You undressed the flesh off of Your soul
To present Your Spirit holy to us
That we might find rest
In these blankets of skin You've chosen to wrap us in
But may we worship like the breaking of a new day
Pulling back these sheets
And unwrapping our hearts like a present
And present them in the presence of our King
May we not be foolish enough to think
That we confine all Your light to one church
Or contain all of Your glory in just one building
Or limit Your grace to one race or denomination
But may our praises be in both spirit and in truth
For our hearts can only beat so fast
These words can only say so much
And the riches of my gaze often falls cheap on Your glory
These hands can only reach so far
Flesh alone will never give You what You fully deserve
So this skin alone will always limit Your worth
So may we not let skin hinder our worship
But paint Your name on the altar of our lips
Stain our words with the color of Your glory
So that whenever we speak about our races
We must acknowledge that You are the one that won them
For there are no colors on our souls
Nothing here but Your fingerprints
For You hold our lives in the same hands that have shaped the world
So may everything that has breath praise Your grip
For You have multiplied Your descendants as numerous as the stars
May our song crescendo with all of creation
As we sing praises to You our Father
The God of all the universe
And every color it has to offer
Since the beginning
You have carved a new song into the heart of every bird
And they are all different

As if You frown on division but give flight to diversity
I pray that our love grows wings
Takes flight in our communities and soars straight toward You
That You might take joy in our worship
That our song would be the soundtrack of You moving here among us
For we are Yours, God,
The medley of Your image
Living by Your script
Living out our differences
And worshiping together
Until we are all together
As one
In the Spirit
Of You

FROM WHENCE MERCIES FLOW

If there is a river
If there is a refreshing that
Flows freely from it
If it does rush, and bank, and wrap
Around the land like an embrace
Of nourishing life
If the river is mighty
And meant to resurrect
The broken, and the weary, and the dry
If the river has life
May it spring up from Your will
That we have written deep
On the yes of our hearts

RUAH

The Wind comes and choreographs the forest
Every tree animated by the gust
Without the Spirit how still is man's journey?
Without the Breath how empty is the dust?

The altar turns offerings to ashes
Our worship is fodder for the fire
Can the flame stay lit without breathing?
Have we forgotten the purpose of the pyre?

The church shines like a city built on a hill
While most people live in the valleys down below
Without laborers what good is the harvest?
How can they hear unless we're willing to go?

The Spirit of God groans within creation
Perhaps even in the people of Jesus
If the people cry that they cannot breathe
Could the breath of God be what they're in need of?

ZION, PART TWO

When we see the light
And our own bodies shine brilliant, beaming newborn beautiful
When we trade back the dust we were formed in
To be refashioned into beings made of nothing but His image
    and His love
Made of nothing but amens and hallelujahs
Creatures of life and breath
Forever intimate with the one who lives and breathes

When we see each other
When we get our first real glimpse at what humanity was intended to be
    since the beginning
When the treasure of ourselves is no longer hidden
When we see the treasure that drove God to digging

What prompted His pursuit
What wouldn't let Him relent
He who didn't avoid cross, or the wear of wounds to find us

When we see ourselves as sons and daughters
And the enormous value that God paid for our purchase
When we see the immense love that He has for us, that's so large
It makes all our past disagreements seem microscopic,
    and we can't find any microscopes here
When we see ourselves, as the bearers of God's image
And the anthem of His truth fills every atom of our being

We will sing

"So long, shadow
There's too much light here for you to trail behind us
Goodbye lies
We're all one here
So you can't divide us
Goodbye division, and racism, and sexism, and fears
Goodbye tears
Our God has wiped you all away"

PENTECOST

He said be
And everything became so
And in the amount of time it took for breath to pass through lips
A universe boomed, and stars sparked, and worlds began to exist
And all became His

He said breathe
And we became lungs
And we became bodies filled to life
Animated by spirit and instruction
And suddenly this dust had a Father
So we became daughters and sons
And love became both our names and our heritage

He said taste and see
He said faith and believe
He said inhale love's promises
And exhale whatever lies lead our hearts to lonely

We went astray
Smoke filled our lungs
Sin cut off our airways
Like a knee to the neck
We cried, I can't breathe
There was no justice, there was no peace

Could He speak again?
Could His Spirit whistle through the caverns of our chests?
Could He send a savior to resuscitate?

They whip His skin
He gasps in pain
He breathes His last
He lay in grave
The Spirit comes
He rises to reign!
He breathes on the church
We rise the same

He says breathe
And we come alive
He says receive
And let Spirit guide
The world needs life
The breath of Christ
Is in our lungs
Say Spirit come!
Say Spirit come!
Spirit come!

We pray . . . Holy Spirit come!

AND STILL...HOPE

Hope comes
Like the first moment
Of morning
When the sun seeps through the sky
To wake a dreaming earth
When day declares an end
To the night
And a chance
To begin all over again

INFORMAL INVITATION

Where has Your presence gone
That has not been made holy?
What has Your Spirit filled
And not left a temple in its wake?
We wake to empty days without You
We've seen the end results of our running
The finish line of our futility has no prize to be won

But once You move
Everything changes
The bound become chainless
The scarred become stainless
You sent a moving Son
One that rose,
And was set,
But the night of death
Couldn't stop it from rising again

And just like that
The locks fell off
And the doors swung off their hinges
And the gates lost their grip
And flew every direction away from here
As if they'd been waiting to become wings
This whole time

And just like that
The path became straight
And lights began to illuminate each step back home
And our feet became holy
And the road started running to us

And suddenly
We couldn't find distance anywhere we looked
Suddenly
Nothing could keep us away from home
Away from You

Come kingdom
Come Spirit
Come soon

LUMINOUS

Night is not the only darkness we know
Not the only ending that chases us without ceasing
We don't have moons and stars for every shadow that hangs
    over our heads
But sometimes
A laugh
A warm hug
The Spirit of God shining through a stranger's smile
Are bright enough to turn even the darkest of depressions
Into a midnight sky
Glittering with hope

ZION, PART THREE

When the story ends,
But the pages keep turning
And we all walk away from the grave like
Resurrection was contagious
Like calendars in the kingdom
Call everyday Easter
And we all get to join in on the celebration

When the story ends,
But the pages keep turning
When on earth sequels as it is in heaven
A new creation springing up from the old one
As if our world were a perfect recipe for the kingdom
And the only ingredient we forgot to add was the King

When the story ends,
But the pages keep turning
And the Hero takes His rightful place in our hearts
When death gets cut from the script, and nothing brings us to tears
    but joy
When paradise invades our old cities
And the kingdom makes a home out of our old homes
And the presence of God turns everything we've ever known into Zion
Oh Zion
When we finally realize how much of heaven
Could have rested in our restless world

We will sing

"So long, shadow
There's too much light here for you to follow
So long, hatred
We'll leave you to the past as we build tomorrow
Goodbye doubt, and fear, and selfish ways
One of these days
Our God will wipe you all away"